Glimpses of the Carmelite Way

MARK DAVIS

Photographs by
GED BARROW

Published by
Rockpool Publishing Ltd.
2b Marine Park
West Kirby
Wirral CH48 5HW
United Kingdom

ISBN 978-0-9554578-0-7

First published 2007

Design and page layout by Jim Poynton
Impressions
The Old Bank
Oxton
Wirral CH43 5SP
United Kingdom

Printed in Thailand

To Mother Mary Assumpta OCD
of the Birkenhead Monastery
who first showed me the beauty of Carmel

CONTENTS

FOREWORD

This remarkable book is to be enjoyed at leisure and pondered prayerfully. True to its title, it offers 'glimpses of the Carmelite way' as seen through the eyes of someone profoundly captivated by his discovery of Carmel's deep spirituality – something he is eager to share with others.

The work itself requires no previous knowledge of Carmelite tradition, only openness to the impact of God's Word and to the writings of Carmel's saints, mystics and Doctors of the Church. A brief introduction outlines the history of the Order's modest beginnings and describes its charism, holding as it does the solitary and common life in a delicate balance. Deeply rooted in the Bible, the leading themes of Carmelite spirituality – their depth, variety and richness – are gradually revealed both through carefully chosen excerpts from the great classics of Carmelite literature and some beautiful original photographs taken by a friend and colleague of the author.

Though the specialist will find in these pages a deep pool of inspiration, this delightful book is not just for Carmelites. It will also be of great interest to those who are not yet familiar with the riches of the tradition and the great universal themes it both illuminates and explores. In the words of Thomas Merton: 'There is no member of the Church who does not owe something to Carmel.'

To savour this book is to embark on a marvellous voyage of discovery from the first stirrings of the human heart in search of the Divine – through the darkness of faith to the final transformation of love in union with God. The author invites us to undertake such a journey with open hearts and open minds in what he calls 'the gentle tradition of Our Lady'.

James McCaffrey, OCD

Unlike many other Religious Orders, the Carmelite family finds its origins not with a particularly inspired individual, but with a group. Its founding story identifies a collection of essentially solitary souls, in the late 12th or early 13th Century, coming to the same location to seek intimacy with God. From this distance, they appear to have been drawn into a corporate life as much by proximity as by intention. They came to the same location – a mountain in Northern Israel called 'Carmel' – to become attentive to the Divine.

From these modest beginnings there has grown a worldwide association of friars, sisters and lay people in two closely related spiritual families. Such has been their importance to Western Catholicism that the Carmelite tradition boasts of no fewer than three 'Doctors of the Church' and its great Saints continue to inspire countless others well beyond the boundaries of their religious home.

Yet in a strange way, Carmelite spirituality is not nearly so well known as one might expect. It has always attracted the interest and study of those deliberately looking for spiritual wisdom within the Christian tradition, yet the average 'person in the pew' has only the vaguest notion of what it is about. For many, the term 'Carmelite' simply means - religious sisters living in enclosure who devote their lives to prayer. While this remains an important aspect of what is a living tradition it does not do justice either to its diversity or its universal significance.

An intriguing tension

As someone who has had the privilege of working with the Anglo-Irish Province of the Discalced Carmelite Friars over the last few years, one of the things that I have found particularly interesting is the relationship between the solitary demands of the interior life and the call to community. The primacy of the eremitical call is held in balance with the creation of welcoming places of warmth and hospitality – sacred spaces where people can simply come along and be themselves.

This implicit acknowledgement that we are all separate individuals with a unique relationship to God and yet that we are somehow 'all in this together' has a very contemporary feel to someone like myself whose professional life brings him into contact with a great variety of people from different Christian traditions. It also echoes the needs of wider western society where the cult of the individual, while remaining strong, is beginning to be questioned.

A question of access

In my own life, the attraction of solitude and the demands of the everyday frame a familiar tension and so my own discovery of the Carmelite tradition awakened in me a desire to know more. Yet this 'knowing more' is not as straightforward as it might seem. In answer to my questions about the 'how's, 'why's and 'wherefore's, I was not presented with the kind of clarity that I desired. The reason, I subsequently discovered, is inherent in the nature of the tradition and the religious culture in which it is preserved. There is a wonderful fluidity about it all, often best approached in symbolic rather than discursive form, best understood by immersion rather than speculation from the water's edge.

Nevertheless, I persisted in my enquiry, partly for my own benefit and partly for others like me who would be enriched by some kind of engagement with Carmelite spirituality - if they could just get a handle on it. Traditionally, the accumulated wisdom gathered over the centuries has been approached in a number of ways: through the writings of the Carmelite saints; the images and symbols of the tradition; the particular character of Carmelite houses and, of course, by personal encounter with individual Carmelites who are themselves undertaking the inward journey and the necessary hours of silent prayer. However, each of these routes into the Carmelite way requires more than a passing interest and my normal experience of Church rarely presents to me, even in a watered down state, the fruit of their discoveries.

Something for everyone?

I once asked a group of friars if the wisdom of Carmel was for everyone or just for those called to their way of life. I got a mixed response. On the one hand it was asserted that the treasures of the years were for both the whole Church and the wider world – anyone who was moved to pray would find something of value here. However, there was also an acknowledgement that a profound understanding was only accessible to those who were seriously engaged in a life of prayer.

From a personal point of view, I would never claim to be a contemplative – I spend too much time rushing about from place to place to make that a realistic possibility. Nevertheless I am someone who tries to pray. In this way I am like so many other people, committed to living a Christian life and yet doing so in the world - having to juggle the increasing demands of family and work while attempting to cultivate an interior life.

All I can say about my experience of Carmel is that having spent some time exploring the different sources of wisdom I have already identified, I know that I have been enriched and expanded by the encounter. As much as anything else this seems to have been because I have had my own life-experience illuminated by the contact. I would not pretend to suggest I have done anything but wander around in the foothills of the tradition, yet I am convinced that even this very limited engagement was of great personal value. It was this inspiration that led me to gather the different elements that have come together to form this brief work.

This illuminated work

This book of photographs, Scripture texts and short quotations from Carmelite writers offers the reader a starting point for exploring the spiritual life from a Carmelite perspective. It is arranged according to a number of themes that emerged from an exercise in reflection and conversation undertaken by a mixed group of Carmelites – friars, sisters and lay people. While these few themes, taken from such a rich and ancient tradition, could never be considered complete or exhaustive what I am hoping they will provide is something rather different - 'Glimpses of the Carmelite Way'.

The invitation here is to engage in a reflective spiritual journey through this collection of ideas and images. The photographs have all been taken by my friend and colleague Ged Barrow and are chosen to illustrate the various themes and echo the selected texts. The choices we have made are necessarily subjective but they have been chosen with care. Some are straightforward whereas others are more oblique, requiring a little more thought. If you find yourself wondering at the lack of people in many of the images remember that the Carmelite story has an eremitical dimension. So we are presenting you with the perspective of the solitary observer sifting through their life-experience in search of the Divine Presence.

With this in mind, we are offering you an illuminated book - something to dip into, rather than read from cover to cover at one sitting. Should you find some moments of quiet to sit and ponder, perhaps you will discover within these few pages, something to nurture your heart and spirit.

Mark Davis

Secret Longings

A good place to begin our journey is where the early Carmelites began – with a growing recognition that there is more to life than meets the eye. Like them we discover from experience that there are hidden depths to the human person and, within each of us, a profound yearning for love, peace and freedom.

Through some form of 'spiritual awakening', we begin to see beyond the superficial attractions that have, so far, engaged us. Experienced as dissatisfaction with the life we are presently leading, the deeper hungers of the human heart are gradually unveiled. We are no longer content and yet our dreams remain – strangely extravagant.

In search of ourselves and aware of a deepening need for connection, we seek a resolution to the personal fragmentation that afflicts us, desiring nothing less than wholeness and ultimate meaning.

From somewhere within, the character of life is changed and like an abandoned lover we refuse to be comforted. Life's transcendent quality has become apparent and calls for a conscious response.

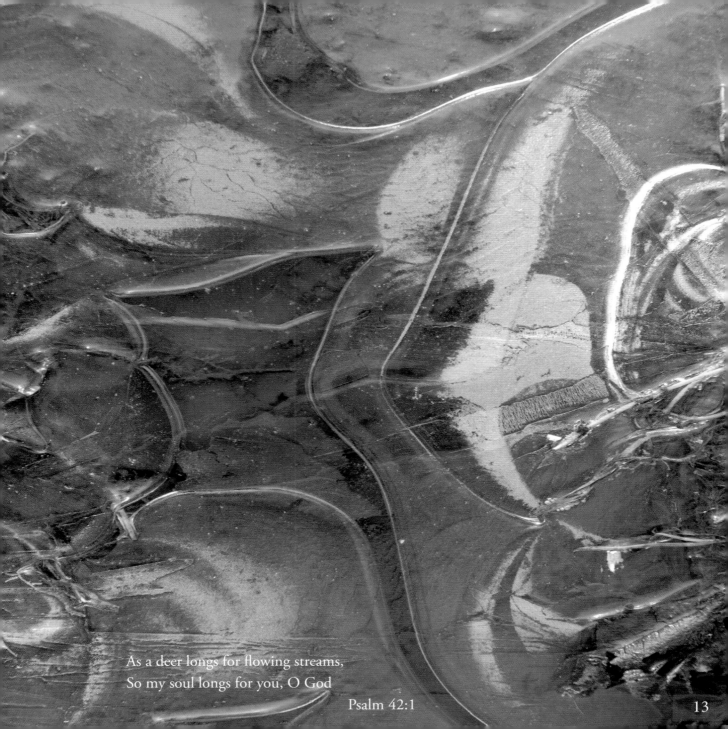

As a deer longs for flowing streams,
So my soul longs for you, O God

Psalm 42:1

13

Give peace to my soul; make it Your heaven,
Your beloved dwelling and Your resting place.
Blessed Elizabeth of the Trinity

The Spiritual Canticle

Where have you hidden,
Beloved, and left me moaning?
You fled like the stag
after wounding me;
I went out calling you, but you were gone.

Shepherds, you who go
up through the sheepfolds to the hill,
if by chance you see
him I love most,
tell him I am sick, I suffer, and I die.

Seeking my Love
I will head for the mountains and for
watersides,
I will not gather flowers,
nor fear wild beasts;
I will go beyond strong men and frontiers.

O woods and thickets,
planted by the hand of my Beloved!
O green meadow,
coated, bright, with flowers,
tell me, has he passed by you?

Pouring out a thousand graces,
he passed these groves in haste;
and having looked at them,
with his image alone,
clothed them in beauty.

St. John of the Cross

Secret Longings

Attentiveness

Through moments of particular insight we glimpse a loving presence pervading the world – a greater love behind the lesser loves with which we have been occupied. Rather than remaining an abstract possibility, the transcendent has become personal; so that it is now someone, rather than something, we are seeking.

But how do we go about it? Even to notice what is stirring requires a certain kind of availability, which is why the Carmelite tradition puts great emphasis on the cultivation of solitude and silence. True attention can only be given if there is space enough inside to be receptive. What is required is a willingness to listen – to listen to other people, to listen to what is happening in the world around us, and perhaps, above all, to listen to ourselves and to what is happening within.

Unstriving but expectant, we acquire a sense of waiting for the unveiling of something that is already there. Through the sifting of experience, often in a favourite 'place of attentiveness', we look for signs of God.

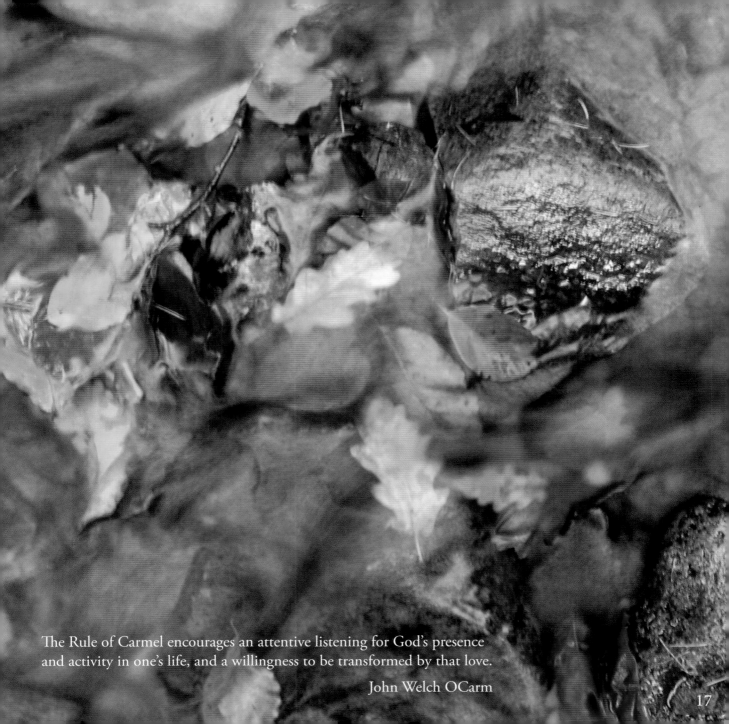

The Rule of Carmel encourages an attentive listening for God's presence
and activity in one's life, and a willingness to be transformed by that love.

John Welch OCarm

Be still and know that I am God

Psalm 46:10

To be attentive means to be present to something, to be aware and open to what is going on. We could speak of 'concentration' if this did not conjure up images of wet towels, furrowed eyebrows and cramming for examinations! To concentrate, however, simply means to focus gently, yet positively, on what we are doing. For most of us that is not easy, since the normal span of human attentiveness is only twenty seconds! To live in the present moment is to experience life and not just to think about it. It is to let life teach us. We can spend so much time and energy imagining all sorts of possible situations, while all the time life itself is passing us by. The magic of the present moment eludes us because we are still trapped in the past or fearful of the future. Jesus directs us not to worry about tomorrow: "Today's trouble is enough today" (Matt 6:34). The same advice could apply to the past as well.

Eugene McCaffrey OCD

Attentiveness

The Sound
of God
Approaching

The invitation to 'seek' prior to finding is deeply embedded in Christian tradition. The One we are looking for is not immediately obvious and both perseverance and patience are required as we wait for God's transforming self-disclosure.

Yet it is not that God wishes to remain hidden forever. In time we discover that He is already actively pursuing us. Though we may have begun to seek for God, He has already taken the initiative. Loving us into life, we are now invited into a conscious relationship.

Many images evoke a sense of the approaching God but those that are favoured in Carmelite thought suggest a gentle, respectful proximity. The 'still small voice' experienced by the prophet Elijah in the biblical 'First Book of Kings', for example, is a favourite text for Carmelites. In this story, the drama of earthquake, storm and fire give way to the relative intimacy of a gentle breeze.

Along with the early friars we can perhaps imagine ourselves as scattered sheep listening out for 'the shepherd's whistle' calling us back to Himself.

If the soul is seeking God,
so much more is God seeking the soul.

St. John of the Cross

Truly God was in this place and I did not know it

Genesis 28:16

There came a mighty wind, so strong
it tore the mountains and shattered the
rocks before Yahweh. But Yahweh was
not in the wind. After the wind came an
earthquake. But Yahweh was not in the
earthquake. After the earthquake came
a fire. But Yahweh was not in the fire.
And after the fire there came the sound
of a gentle breeze. And when Elijah
heard this, he covered his face with his
cloak and went out and stood at the
entrance of the cave.

1 Kings 19:11-13

The Sound of God
Approaching

Pray As
You Can

Carmelite tradition does not insist in a particular way of praying. The invitation is simply to pray. What is essential is the cultivation of a relationship with the personal God you are discovering. Because every relationship is unique, the idea is to pray in the way that we find easiest and most meaningful.

Prayer can take various forms and there is no right or wrong way of doing it. The real challenge is to keep at it – to be present, available and open. What we may discover, however, is that there are certain places in which it can flourish – perhaps your kitchen, your garden or some favourite chapel or Cathedral.

While there is truth in the saying that 'in prayer we are all beginners', there is, nevertheless, a journey to be undertaken. Although the route we take may be very different from that of others, the destination is the same. But what we discover, as we make progress, is that one way of praying gives way to another. We move from room to room in what St. Teresa of Avila called, our 'interior castle' – always seeking the indwelling God.

In the morning, long before dawn, he got up and left the house and went off to a lonely place and prayed there.

Mark 1:31

25

Prayer in my opinion
is nothing else than
an intimate sharing
between friends; it
means taking time
frequently to be alone
with Him who we
know loves us.

St. Teresa of Avila

I do not have the courage to force myself
to search out beautiful prayers in books.
There are so many of them it really gives
me a headache and each prayer is more
beautiful than the others. I cannot recite
them all and not knowing which to choose,
I do like children who do not know how
to read, I say very simply to God what I
wish to say, without composing beautiful
sentences, and He always understands me.
For me, prayer is an aspiration of the heart;
it is a simple glance directed to heaven, it is
a cry of gratitude and love in the midst of
trial as well as joy; finally, it is something
great, supernatural, which expands my soul
and unites me to Jesus.

St. Thérèse of Lisieux

Pray As You Can

Pondering
the Word

The self-disclosure of God to the human person takes many forms. Yet, over the centuries, men and women, rich and poor, educated or uneducated, attest to being 'spoken to' personally through the pages of the Bible. This should not surprise us because our faith is rooted in the story it contains — that of the person of Jesus Christ.

As individual believers or as Christian communities, we seek to 'get to know Jesus' through the pages of the Gospels. This savouring of the sacred text, rather than reading it as an academic exercise, is a living source of prayer and communion. Over time, personal experience bears testimony to an intimate connection between what is happening in and around us and what is written in the Scriptures.

Pondering the Word of God, then, is a vital element in the developing relationship. So strong is this theme in Carmelite life that it occupies a central place in the original 'rule' that describes this way of being Christian. Each Carmelite is urged to stay close to home, recollected in prayer and pondering the Scriptures 'unless attending to some other duty'.

The word of God
is something alive
and active

Hebrews 4 : 12

*Your word is a lamp to
my feet, and a light to
my path*

Psalm 119:105

To hear the voiceless word of God in the gospels, we need a listening ear. It is rare to find someone who really listens. I once met such a person! It was Mother Teresa of Calcutta. When I met her she was washing the face of a leper. Her eyes were fixed on him, his on her. No word passed between them. But this was an alert stillness, an eloquent sharing. Here was someone who was really listening – quiet, fully alive, focussed, attentive. Hers was a listening heart. Her whole bearing was a lesson in total presence….

She glanced at me for a moment with her piercing eyes, then turned back to attend to the leper and said, 'We need the Word of God for this.' I had loved scripture, studied it, taught it, written about it. But here was a woman of deep and simple faith. She really listened to it, lived it and put it into practice. It had borne fruit in her life, not just thirty or sixty but a hundredfold.

James McCaffrey OCD

Pondering the Word

Songs of the Beloved

The spiritual life, according to the saints of Carmel, is primarily an affair of the heart. We seek the 'God of Love' made flesh in Jesus Christ and this is whom we find. It is said of St. Teresa that she 'fell in love with God' and wished that others would do the same.

Somewhere along the way we share in this transforming experience, as it is revealed to us that we are infinitely beloved. No amount of weakness, half-heartedness or sin can change this startling reality.

The wonder of God's love, then, comes first – something so personal and so tender that Scripture uses the image of 'spousal love' to describe it. No more significant expression can be found to describe the intimate and indissoluble link between God and the people He has created.

While many other texts refer to it, the 'Song of Songs' holds a special place. Though different opinions are proposed as to its meaning, a strong rabbinical tradition suggests that it is simply God's love song to His chosen people and this is what the Carmelite mystics have always believed.

My Beloved lifts up his voice,
he says to me,
"Come then, my love,
my lovely one, come.
 For see, winter is past,
the rains are over and gone.
The flowers appear on the earth.
The season of glad songs has come,
the cooing of the turtledove is heard in our land".

The Song of Songs 2:10-12

Who are you, sweet light, that fills me
and illuminates the darkness of my heart?

St. Edith Stein

34

My Beloved, the mountains,
and lonely wooded valleys,
strange islands,
and resounding rivers,
the whistling of love-stirring breezes,
the tranquil night
at the time of the rising dawn,
silent music,
sounding solitude,
the supper that refreshes,
and deepens love.

St. John of the Cross

Songs of
the Beloved

Freeing
the Heart

In spite of our best intentions, there exists within each of us resistance to the Divine activity. In the language of Carmel, the 'caverns of the human heart' are so deep that only God can fill them, yet they are cluttered up with disordered desires and fragmented appetites. What is required is the breaking of bonds of enslavement so as to make space for God.

What 'enslaves' us may be big or small. According to St. John of the Cross a bird that is tied by a single thread is just as held as one restrained by a rope — they both need to be broken if the bird is to fly. In his view even 'good things', can become unhelpful. These 'lesser loves' can choke the heart and prevent the Divine union for which we were created.

But how can such cords be severed? How can lesser loves be left behind? Only through prayer with the help of the Holy Spirit who 'enflames the soul with love for God'.

Only if a greater love is experienced can we break free from whatever holds us fast.

How will a person brought to birth and nurtured in a world of small horizons rise up to you Lord, if you do not raise him by your hand which made him?

St. John of the Cross

To be detached from all the things
of life is to live in the greatest calm.

St. Teresa of Avila

When night comes
and you look back
over the day

and see how
fragmentary
it has been,

and how much
you planned that
has gone undone,

and all the reasons
you have been
embarrassed
and ashamed:

Just take everything
exactly as it is,

put it into God's
hands and leave
it to Him.

then you will be
able to rest in Him
really rest

and start the next day
as a new life.

St. Edith Stein

Freeing the Heart

Living Water

Many Biblical texts speak of water that is 'living' – in that it gives life, renews and invigorates. Sparkling in the lives of those who wash or drink, this primordial element expresses the exuberant generosity and abundance of God's love.

Within this ancient spiritual tradition, water has always been a potent image of prayer and the interior life. So much so that St. Teresa of Avila used it as a way of describing different stages in a life of prayer. Imagining the soul as a garden in need of cultivation, she emphasised the necessity of watering the 'good seed'. Starting with our own efforts in drawing water from a deep well, the garden is eventually watered by the Lord Himself through the provision of welcome rain.

In similar vein, St. John of the Cross uses water in his poetry to describe the bountiful providence of an inflowing God. Even today, within each Carmelite house, the inward movement of the Holy Spirit is given physical symbolic expression in the form of a bubbling fountain through which water constantly flows.

Jesus stood there and cried out:
"Let anyone who is thirsty come to me!
Let anyone who believes in me come and drink!"
As Scripture says, "From his heart shall flow
streams of living water."

John 7:37-38

Contemplation is nothing but a hidden, peaceful, loving inflow of God. If it is given room, it will enflame the spirit with love.

St. John of the Cross

O Life, who gives life to all!
Do not deny me this sweetest water
that You promise to those who want
it. I want it, Lord, and I beg for it,
and I come to You.
Don't hide Yourself, Lord, from me,
since You know my need and that
this water is the true medicine for a
soul wounded with love of You.
O Lord, how many kinds of fire
there are in this life!   Oh, how true
it is that one should live in fear!
Some kinds of fire consume the soul,
other kinds purify it that it might
live ever rejoicing in You.
O living founts from the wounds of
my God, how you have flowed with
great abundance for our sustenance,
and how surely he who strives to
sustain himself with this divine
liqueur will advance in the midst of
the dangers of this life.

St. Teresa of Avila

Living Water

In the
Footsteps
of Mary

In the early days of the Order, 'The Rule of St. Albert' specified that there be an oratory in the middle of the hermit cells. The early community chose to dedicate this church to the Mother of Jesus. She thus became 'The Lady of the Place' which, in medieval culture, amounted to a request to be under her patronage.

Their choice was made because in the Gospels, Mary stood out for the first friars as a figure of humble acceptance to the kind purposes of God. Her hidden life echoed their own, showing humanity at its most mysterious and most triumphant.

Unsurprisingly, therefore, Carmelites have always been particularly devoted to Mary – steadfast in their belief that she was looking after them. All their greatest saints bore testament to this. St. Thérèse of Lisieux, for example, wrote of her deep familiar relationship with the one whom she described as 'more Mother than Queen'.

When we visit Carmelite houses today it is difficult not to be impressed by their hospitality and warmth — open hearts and open homes in the gentle tradition of Our Lady.

"I am the handmaid of the Lord", said Mary,
"let what you have said be done to me".

Luke 1:38

Only a few words from the
Virgin Mary have come down
to us in the Gospels. But these
few words are like heavy grains
of pure gold. When they melt in
the ardour of loving meditation,
they more than suffice to bathe
our entire lives in a luminous
golden glow.
St. Edith Stein

The devotion to Mary is one of the most delightful flowers in Carmel's garden. I should like to call it a sunflower. This flower rises high above the other flowers. Borne aloft on a tall stem, rich in green leaves, the flower is raised yet higher from among the green foliage.

It is characteristic of this flower to turn itself towards the sun and moreover it is an image of the sun. It is a simple flower: it can grow in all gardens and it is an ornament to all. It is tall and firm and has deep roots like a tree…

The flower itself represents the soul created after God's image in order to absorb the sunlight of God's bounty…

Such a flower was Mary. Like her, so may we, flowers from her seed, raise our flower buds to the sun who infused Himself into her and will transmit to us also the beams of His light and warmth.

Blessed Titus Brandsma

In the Footsteps of Mary

One Dark Night

The inward journey is not always characterised by peace and light. After a period of fair weather during which prayer is satisfying and God feels very close, most people encounter darkness – suffering, dryness and confusion.

If we do not know how to respond, we can easily become discouraged and abandon our prayer. This is where the Carmelite tradition, and especially St. John of the Cross, has a special contribution to make. What he holds out to us is both an understanding of our predicament and the encouragement to continue.

Provided that the discomfiture is not from our deliberate fault, this darkness is not what it appears. Rather than a setback, it is, in reality, an invitation. Under cover of this protective night God comes closer still, cleansing, healing and purifying.

Thus, for one who perseveres in prayer, this frightening darkness is transformed. It becomes the 'glad night' of John's famous poem – a place of meeting between the soul and her Beloved.

Lord, let me walk blindly on the path
you have traced out for me.
I do not seek to understand your way:
I am your child;
wisdom's font and Father,
You are my Father too.
Your road may lead through darkness,
but it will lead to you

(attributed to) St. Edith Stein

49

O living flame of love
that tenderly wounds my soul

St. John of the Cross

One dark night,
fired with love's urgent longings
- ah, the sheer grace! -
I went out unseen,
my house being now all stilled…

On that glad night
in secret, for no one saw me,
nor did I look at anything
with no other light or guide
than the one that burned in my heart.

This guided me
more surely than the light of noon
to where he was awaiting me
- him I knew so well -
there in a place where no one appeared.

O guiding night!
O night more lovely than the dawn!
O night that has united
the Lover with his beloved,
transforming the beloved in her Lover.

St. John of the Cross

One

Dark

Night

Surrender

The paradox of surrender is at the heart of Christian experience and is a major theme throughout the spiritual journey — reflecting as it does the passion, death and resurrection of Jesus Christ. For on the Cross of Calvary, Christ opened his arms to the world and offered His life – before rising in triumph on Easter morning.

What we increasingly realise is that the perfection we seek can only be achieved by a radical self-giving. Yet this is often the last thing we desire — something to be embraced when all other alternatives are exhausted.

However, when experienced, what looks like a kind of death, is really the key to new life. The gift of self, to others and to Christ, expands our hearts and increases our capacity to give and receive love. Played out in the personal and collective circumstances of our lives, each wilful act of surrender unites us more closely with God. A point is reached where we no longer place any conditions on the relationship and so become transparent to His kindness.

Unless a grain of wheat falls to the ground
and dies, it remains but a single grain; but
if it dies it yields a rich harvest

John 12:24

Jesus does not demand great actions from us but simply surrender and gratitude.

St. Thérèse of Lisieux

To use an analogy, we could say that, at first, her hand was held with palm downward and fingers clenched, seeking to grasp as best they could. Then, with the passage of time and a change of attitude and perspective, her fingers relaxed gradually and eventually released their hold, while her hand turned until her palm was outstretched, ready to offer and to receive much in return. It took Thérèse almost her entire lifetime to reach this point.

Conrad De Meester OCD

(describing gradual surrender in the life of St. Thérèse of Lisieux)

Surrender

Compassion

Friendship with Jesus Christ reveals to us a Divine presence whose essential nature is characterised by mercy and forgiveness. The Gospel stories are filled with potent images of a personal God who is reckless in compassion – a suffering servant, a forgiving father and a devoted shepherd who lays down his life for his sheep.

It will not surprise us to discover, therefore, that the circle of concern embraced by Carmelites is not confined to those close by, but is drawn on a wider canvas. Even for those parts of the Carmelite family living in enclosure, the personal inward struggle is undertaken, in some mysterious way, on behalf of the whole of humanity.

Our own developing intimacy with God creates in us a deep empathy for those in need and an acute desire for the transformation of society as well as the individual. As part of a praying community in the midst of the world, at home or attached to a local church, we will increasingly want to be in solidarity with the poor and the dispossessed.

Come, you whom my Father has blessed, take for your heritage the kingdom prepared for you since the foundation of the world. For I was hungry and you gave me food; I was thirsty and you gave me drink; I was a stranger and you made me welcome; naked and you clothed me, sick and you visited me, in prison and you came to see me.

Matthew 25:34-36

In the evening of life you will be examined in love.   St John of the Cross

Christ has no body now
on earth but yours,
no hands but yours,
no feet but yours.
Yours are the eyes
through which looks out
Christ's compassion
on the world.
Yours are the feet
with which Christ
is to go about doing good.
Yours are the hands
with which He is to bless
people today.

(attributed to) St Teresa of Avila

Compassion

Communities
of Faith

For each individual, the spiritual
journey is unique and personal but it
is not without companions. Though
the early Carmelites were drawn to
the solitary life of the hermit, creating
contemplative communities has always
been part of their essential call.

But as with any community, domestic or
religious, living together may not be an
untroubled activity. Those closest to us
constitute the immediate context of our
journey in faith. Either by accident or
design they support and challenge us in
our desire to grow in love. According
to St. John of the Cross they are the
craftsmen used by God to chisel us into
shape.

In its various forms the Carmelite
model involves trying to live in loving
harmony as brothers or sisters.
Though the eremitical call implies
the primacy of personal space, the
tradition has always attached great
importance to the sharing of life and
prayer with others. Indeed, St Teresa
believed that practical loving care
for one another was a measure of the
authenticity of the life of prayer.

All must be friends, all must be loved,
all must be held dear, all must be helped

I give you a new commandment – love one another;
just as I have loved you, you also must love one another.
By this love you have for one another,
everyone will know that you are my disciples.

John 13:34-35

From the beginning of this tradition
in Palestine, life with others has been
an integral component of Carmelite
spirituality. Time has only strengthened
the value of living as a community. Every
reform worked to shore up the foundations
of community life.

As elementary as living together and
praying together seems, the witness of
such a community can be one of the most
powerful actions on behalf of a more just
and peaceful world…

A vital community life lived in friendship
and equality gives witness to the possibility
of a world where men and women can live
in harmony. If this community can share
its gifts and resources, and live simply, it
makes attractive the possibility of alternate
forms of living not based on power, money
or prestige…

The Carmelite tradition brings to the
struggle a simple, but powerful resource: a
prayerful community of friends.

John Welch OCarm

Communities
of Faith

Union
with God

The vision of humanity presented to us in the Carmelite way is nothing less than the belief that 'union with God' is possible even in this life.

The path to this blessed state is presented through a variety of images including ascending a mountain, crossing a desert or seeking the centre of a castle made of crystal. What each points to is a moment of arrival where God Himself is embraced in a final mutual act of love and surrender.

The journey has been both joyous and costly. Perfect surrender is only accomplished through the lesser surrenders that have led to this place; deep communion is only realised through fidelity to prayer and perfect love emerges from the daily effort to love unconditionally.

The witness of Carmel is that there is a sunlit upland, beyond the darkest of nights and that this is available even to us. The promise and the invitation hold true and the human person is fulfilled. To people so transformed, the door to eternity is already ajar.

Flame, living flame, compelling,
yet tender past all telling,
reaching the secret centre of my soul!
Since now evasion's over,
finish your work, my Lover,
break the last thread,
wound me and make me whole!

St. John of the Cross

This, then, is what I pray, kneeling before
the Father,
from whom every family, whether spiritual
or natural, takes its name:
Out of His infinite glory, may he give you
the power through his Spirit
for your hidden self to grow strong,
so that Christ may live in your hearts
through faith,
and then, planted in love and built on love,
you will, with all the saints,
have strength to grasp the breadth
and the length, the height and the depth;
until, knowing the love of Christ,
which is beyond all knowledge,
you are filled with the utter fullness of God.

Ephesians 3:14-19

Union with God

Should you wish to find out more about the Carmelite family please make use of the following portals:

The Carmelite Forum in Britain and Ireland: ...... www.carmeliteforum.org

Carmelite Institute of Britain and Ireland .... www.cibi.ie

Discalced (Teresian) Carmelites OCD

OCD Friars English Region: .... www.carmelite.org.uk

OCD Friars Irish-Scottish Region: .... www.ocd.ie

Carmelite Nuns UK: .... www.carmelnuns.org.uk

Carmelite Sisters Ireland: .... www.carmelitesister.ie

OCDS Secular Order UK: .... www.carmelite.org.uk

OCDS Secular Order Ireland: .... www.ocd.ie/secular

Carmelites Order (Ancient Observance) O Carm

O Carm Friars UK: .... www.carmelite.org

O Carm Friars Ireland: .... www.carmelites.ie

O Carm Lay Carmel: .... www.laycarmel.org

The Leaven Carmelite Secular Institute .... www.carmelite.org

ACKNOWLEDGMENTS

Editions used and the symbols to denote them:

Works by St. Teresa of Avila
The Collected Works of St. Teresa of Avila, 3 vols, tr. Kieran Kavanaugh, OCD & Otilio Rodriguez, OCD, Washington, DC: ICS Publications, 1987, 1980 & 1985, including:

IC	*Interior Castle*
Life	*The Book of Her Life*
Sp Test	*Spiritual Testimonies*
Sol	*Soliloquies*
WP	*The Way of Perfection*

Works by St. John of the Cross
The Collected Works of Saint John of the Cross, tr. Kieran Kavanaugh, OCD & Otilio Rodriguez, OCD, Washington, DC: ICS Publications, 1991, including:

A	*The Ascent of Mount Carmel*
DN	*The Dark Night*
LF	*The Living Flame of Love*
SC	*The Spiritual Canticle*
SLL	*The Sayings of Light and Love*

Works by St. Thérèse of Lisieux

SS	*Story of a Soul: The Autobiography of St. Thérèse of Lisieux,* tr. John Clarke, OCD Washington DC: ICS Publications, 1996

Works by St. Edith Stein

SEL	*Edith Stein; Selected Writings,* tr. Susanne M Batzdorff, Sprinfield, IL: Templegate, 1990
HL	*Edith Stein; The Hidden Life,* Washington, DC: ICS Publications, 1992
W	*Essays on Woman* (The Collected Works of Edith Stein, II), tr. Frida Mary Oben, Washington DC: ICS Publications, 1996

Works by Blessed Elizabeth of the Trinity

CW	*The Complete Works of Elizabeth of the Trinity,* vol. 1, Washington DC: ICS Publications, 1984.

All the above are used with permission from Washington Province of Discalced Carmelites, ICS Publications, 2131 Lincoln Road, N.E. Washington, DC 20002-1199 U.S.A. www.icspublications.org

Other Works (All used with permission)

TCW	*The Carmelite Way,* John Welch OCarm, 'Gracewing' Fowler Wright Books, (1996),
PP	*Patterns of Prayer,* Eugene McCaffrey OCD (1992), Paulist Press Inc., New York, Mahwah, N.J., USA.
CC	James McCaffrey OCD, *The Carmelite Charism – exploring the biblical roots,* (2004) Veritas Publications, Dublin.
CMHS	*Carmelite Mysticism Historical Sketches,* Titus Brandsma O.Carm., (1986) The Carmelite Press, Darien, Illinois, USA.
WEH	Conrad De Meester OCD, *With Empty Hands: The Message of St. Therese of Lisieux,* (2002) Burns & Oates, London and New York.
COL	*Centred On love: The Poems of Saint John of the Cross, translated* by Marjorie Flower OCD (1983), The Carmelite Nuns, Varroville, NSW, Australia.

Biblical Texts

JB	*The Jerusalem Bible,* Darton, Longman and Todd Ltd and Doubleday Inc (1966)
NRSV	*The New Revised Standard Version Bible,* The National Council of Churches of Christ in the USA (1989)

LIST OF QUOTATIONS

Secret Longings

- Psalm 42:1 (NRSV)
- 'Give peace to my soul…' Blessed Elizabeth of the Trinity, *'Prayer to the Trinity' CW p.183*
- 'Where have you hidden…' St. John of the Cross, SC Stanzas 1-5

Attentiveness

- 'The rule of Carmel…' John Welch OCarm, TCW p.171
- Psalm 46:10 (NRSV)
- 'To be attentive…' Eugene McCaffrey OCD, PP p.46

The Sound of God Approaching

- 'If the soul…' St. John of the Cross, LF 3.28
- Genesis 28:16 (JB)
- I Kings 19: 11-13 (JB)

Pray As You Can

- Mark 1:35 (JB)
- 'Prayer, in my opinion…' St. Teresa of Avila, Life Ch.8 par 5
- 'I do not have the courage…' St. Thérèse of Lisieux, SS (Manuscript B) p.242

Pondering the Word

- Psalm 119:105 (NRSV)
- 'To hear the voiceless…' James McCaffrey OCD, CC p.25

Songs of the Beloved

- The Song of Songs 2:10-12 (JB)
- 'My Beloved, the mountains…' St. John of the Cross, SC Stanzas 14-15
- 'Who are you…' St. Edith Stein, SEL p.93

Freeing the Heart

- 'How will a person…' St. John of the Cross, SLL 26
- 'To be detached…' St. Teresa of Avila, Life Ch.35 par 12
- 'When night comes…' St. Edith Stein, W p.145

Living Water

- John 7:37-38 (JB)
- 'Contemplation is…' St. John of the Cross, DN I.10.6
- 'O Life, who gives life…' St. Teresa of Avila, Sol IX:2

In the Footsteps of Mary

- Luke 1:38 (JB)
- 'Only a few words…' St. Edith Stein, HL p.106
- 'The devotion to Mary…' Blessed Titus Brandsma, CMHS, Lecture 4

One Dark Night

- 'Let me walk blindly…' attributed to St. Edith Stein
- 'O Living flame…' St. John of the Cross, LF Stanza 1
- 'One Dark Night…' St. John of the Cross, DN Stanzas 1, 3-5

Surrender

- John 12:24 (JB)
- 'Jesus does not demand…' St. Therese of Lisieux, SS *(Manuscript B)* p.188
- 'To use an analogy…' Conrad De Meester OCD, WEH p. 119

Compassion

- Matthew 25:34 –36 (JB)
- 'In the evening of life…' St. John of the Cross, SLL 60
- 'Christ has no body…' (attributed to) St. Teresa of Avila

Communities of Faith

- 'All must be friends…' St. Teresa of Avila, WP 4.7
- John 13:34-35 (JB)
- *'From the beginning of this tradition…'* John Welch OCarm, TCW p.152-154

Union with God

- 'Flame, living flame…' St. John of the Cross, COL p.22
- Ephesians 3:14-19

INDEX OF PHOTOGRAPHS

Prints of the photographs reproduced
in this book, together with other images by
Ged Barrow, can be purchased by contacting

www.rockpoolpublishing.com

Bubion,
Alpujarra,
Spain

Ref G0608

Nant y Pandy,
Glyndyfrdwy,
Wales

Ref G0615

Hawarden,
Wales.

G0622

Marko's
Workshop,
England

Ref G0609

West Kirby,
England

Ref G0616

West Kirby,
England.

Ref G0623

Iglesia El Salvador,
Nerja,
Spain

Ref G0610

Island of
Middle Eye,
England

Ref G0617

Chester,
England.

Ref G0624

Island of
Middle Eye,
England

Ref G0611

Wirral,
England

Ref G0618

Brest Harbour,
France.

Ref G0625

Nant y Pandy,
Glyndyfrdwy,
Wales

Ref G0612

Birkenhead Docks,
England

Ref G019

Island of Crete,
Greece.

Ref G 0626

Alpujarras,
Sierra Nevada,
Spain

Ref G0613

West Kirby,
England

Ref G0620

Lanjaron,
Alpujarras,
Spain.

Ref G0627

Dee Estuary,
England

Ref G0614

Wirral,
England

Ref G0621

Dee Estuary,
West Kirby,
England.

Ref G0628